Additional FREE Resources

www.questionsaboutme.com/story

ACCESS THE FREE PRINTABLE LIBRARY FOR:

Editable family tree

Replacement and additional questions (short and detailed)

Lined pages to answer questions and insert into the book

Like our Facebook page
@QuestionsAboutMe

Follow us on Instagram
@QuestionsAboutMe_Official

Questions & Customer Service
hello@questionsaboutme.com

Tell Me Your Life Story, Grandpa

by Questions About Me™

www.questionsaboutme.com

table of contents

introduction

This journal was created for you—grandfathers of all kinds, both biological and non-biological—to capture the moments that have shaped your life.

Our legacy and wisdom can only be treasured by future generations if we take the time to share our life stories.

Tell Me Your Life Story, Grandpa serves as a tool to help you write your thoughts, stories, and reflections, turning this guided journal into a priceless treasure to share with your children, loved ones, and future generations.

The engaging, thought-provoking prompts make it simple to record everything from memories of your childhood and life lessons to your hopes for the future.

Once completed, this book will help your children and future generations gain a fuller understanding of your family's origins.

Most valuably, though, this journal will tell your life story. It's what your family will learn about you and will help you connect with them in a meaningful way. This timeless keepsake is also your chance to inspire the next generation and generations to come with your experiences, accomplishments, and life lessons.

getting the most out of this journal

Just remember there are no strict rules for using or completing this guided journal.

The format of this book is flexible, and the questions can be tackled in any way. Start from anywhere you like, and fill in your answers in any order. You can skip around and answer questions, or you can start at the beginning and work through them in order.

There is no right or wrong way to respond to each question. You may choose not to answer some questions, and some questions may simply not apply to you. Feel free to use the additional questions available from our website in place of these questions.

Try not to overthink or hold back when answering the questions; instead, write freely and record whatever comes into your mind and heart. Where possible, try to be honest, thoughtful, and detailed in the answers you give to all the questions. There's no need to be formal or worry about structuring your answer perfectly. The best answers are the ones that are unedited and come straight from your heart.

HINT

Be specific wherever you can be. Precise details help make your story come alive. Use both first and last names wherever possible. Also, try for as many exact dates, locations, and addresses, as well as brand names, etc. as possible. Try writing "... the mist-green 1950 Chevy" instead of "...Dad's car," and "...pink peonies" instead of "...flowers." Try "... at Starbucks on Seventh Street, downtown" rather than just "... at Starbucks" to paint a clear picture with your words.

Take your time with answering the questions. As there are a lot of questions, you may want to complete the book over multiple sessions, perhaps dedicating some time each day over a period of weeks or months to complete them.

You may even find it enjoyable to have a family member help set up a video camera or audio recording equipment and have them ask you the questions out loud then record your answers.

If you need additional space to answer a question, you can utilize the extra notes pages at the end of each section. You can also use the notes pages to answer the replacement or additional questions from our website or use them as a space to include some memorable photos.

Go easy on yourself and enjoy the process!

•••

my details
& time capsule

my details

FULL NAME

DATE OF BIRTH

PLACE
OF BIRTH

EYE
COLOR

HEIGHT

HAIR
COLOR

DISTINGUISHING
MARKS

ATTACH YOUR BABY PHOTO HERE

time capsule

TODAY'S DATE

POPULATION OF YOUR CITY	POPULATION OF YOUR COUNTRY
LEADER OF YOUR COUNTRY	POPULATION OF THE WORLD

THE PRICE OF...

GALLON/BOTTLE OF MILK	MAGAZINE
CUP OF COFFEE	BOOK
LOAF OF BREAD	MORTGAGE INTEREST RATE
GALLON OF GAS/ LITRE OF PETROL	AVERAGE WEEKLY WAGE
POSTAGE STAMP	MONTHLY RENT/ MORTGAGE PAYMENT
NEWSPAPER	AVERAGE HOUSE PRICE

CUT AND ATTACH A NEWSPAPER
MASTHEAD FROM TODAY

•••

early years

Were you named after anyone?

_____

_____

_____

_____

_____

_____

Do you like or dislike your name? Why?

_____

_____

_____

_____

_____

_____

If you could choose a different name, what would it be?

_____

_____

_____

_____

_____

_____

How old were your parents when you were born?

_____

_____

_____

_____

Are there any stories you were told about your birth?

_____

_____

_____

_____

_____

_____

_____

_____

_____

_____

_____

_____

_____

_____

_____

_____

_____

Were you a healthy baby, or were there health concerns?

_____

_____

_____

_____

_____

_____

_____

_____

_____

_____

_____

_____

_____

What are some stories your parents have shared
with you about when you were a baby?

_____

_____

_____

_____

_____

_____

_____

_____

_____

What is your earliest memory?

_____

_____

_____

_____

_____

_____

_____

_____

_____

_____

_____

_____

_____

_____

_____

_____

_____

_____

What was the same or different about the way you were cared for as
a baby compared to the way your own parents were cared for?

_____

_____

_____

_____

_____

_____

_____

_____

_____

_____

_____

_____

_____

_____

_____

What do you know about the house you lived in
as a baby? How long did you live there?

_____

_____

_____

_____

_____

_____

_____

_____

_____

_____

_____

_____

_____

_____

_____

Describe a character or personality trait you inherited from each (or either) of your parents. Be sure to state which parent for each trait.

_____

_____

_____

_____

_____

_____

_____

_____

_____

_____

_____

_____

_____

_____

_____

_____

_____

_____

_____

_____

_____

_____

_____

_____

_____

_____

_____

_____

_____

notes

notes

childhood

Did you have special toys or items that were precious to you, and what's the story of how they came to you?

_____

_____

_____

_____

_____

_____

_____

What type of games did you enjoy playing with your friends, siblings, or on your own?

_____

_____

_____

_____

_____

_____

_____

What childhood fears do you remember having? For example, did you think there were monsters under the bed, or were you afraid of stepping on cracks?

_____

_____

_____

_____

_____

_____

_____

_____

What are some nostalgic smells, sounds, or tastes
that bring you back to childhood?

_____

_____

_____

_____

_____

_____

_____

_____

Describe places where you spent most of your free time when
you were little. Your room? Your backyard? A friend's house?

_____

_____

_____

_____

_____

_____

_____

_____

_____

_____

Did you have your own room growing up?

_____

_____

_____

_____

_____

_____

_____

What did you like or dislike about the area(s) you lived growing up?

_____

_____

_____

_____

_____

_____

_____

_____

What were mealtimes like growing up? Was there a strict routine?

_____

_____

_____

_____

_____

_____

_____

_____

Describe your childhood kitchen—the smells,
tastes, sounds, textures, and colors.

_____

_____

_____

_____

_____

_____

_____

_____

_____

Were there any foods you disliked as a child,
and do you still dislike them today?

_____

_____

_____

_____

_____

_____

_____

Did you have regular chores to do at home, and
how did you feel about this at the time?

_____

_____

_____

_____

_____

_____

_____

_____

_____

Other than your parents, were there any other adult role models
in your childhood? What made them important to you?

_____

_____

_____

_____

_____

_____

_____

_____

_____

What is an activity you used to do with your parents? State
whether it was something you did with either one parent or both,
and describe a memory of enjoying that activity together.

_____

_____

_____

_____

_____

_____

_____

_____

_____

_____

_____

_____

_____

_____

_____

_____

Did you feel connected to *both* of your parents growing
up or one more than the other? Why or why not?

_____

_____

_____

_____

_____

_____

_____

_____

_____

Did your family have any struggles that had to be overcome? Did they try to shield you from them, or did you play an active role in overcoming them?

_____

_____

_____

_____

_____

_____

_____

_____

_____

_____

_____

Were you given an allowance? If so, can you remember
how much it was? What did you spend it on?

_____

_____

_____

_____

_____

_____

Did you have enough money growing up?

_____

_____

_____

_____

_____

_____

_____

_____

_____

How did you handle peer pressure when you were growing up?

_____

_____

_____

_____

_____

_____

_____

_____

_____

_____

Can you recall some of the comments made by teachers
on your report cards about your behavior or academic
ability? What was your opinion on these comments?

_____

_____

_____

_____

_____

_____

_____

_____

_____

_____

_____

What subject did you wish was taught in school?

_____

_____

_____

_____

_____

What were your favorite subjects in school?

_____
_____
_____
_____
_____
_____
_____
_____
_____
_____
_____

Did you play any sports or instruments, or participate
in any extracurricular school activities?

_____
_____
_____
_____
_____
_____
_____
_____
_____

Which sports teams were you a fan of as a child?

_____
_____
_____
_____
_____
_____
_____
_____
_____

Describe a standout memory or memories from your high school years.

_____
_____
_____
_____
_____
_____
_____
_____
_____
_____
_____
_____
_____
_____
_____

Describe a proud achievement during your childhood or teenage years.

_____
_____
_____
_____
_____
_____
_____
_____
_____
_____
_____
_____
_____
_____
_____

What do you remember most about summertime and
other times you were out of school as a kid?

_____

_____

_____

_____

_____

_____

_____

_____

_____

Did you have a best friend or a close group of friends? Do you
still keep in contact with any of your school friends today?

_____

_____

_____

_____

_____

_____

_____

_____

_____

_____

_____

_____

_____

_____

_____

_____

_____

Did you have any friends whom your parents disapproved of?
What caused their disapproval?

_____

_____

_____

_____

_____

_____

_____

_____

_____

How were you disciplined when you did something to upset
your parents? What did you do when you got in trouble?

_____

_____

_____

_____

_____

_____

_____

_____

_____

_____

_____

_____

_____

_____

_____

_____

Did you go on family vacations? If so, what memories do you have of them?

_____

_____

_____

_____

_____

_____

_____

_____

_____

_____

_____

_____

_____

_____

_____

_____

_____

_____

_____

_____

_____

_____

_____

_____

_____

_____

_____

_____

_____

_____

_____

What special dates did your family celebrate each
year? How did you celebrate them?

_____

_____

_____

_____

_____

_____

Is there a particular childhood birthday party or other celebration
that stands out in your memory? Why does it stand out?

_____

_____

_____

_____

_____

_____

_____

Do you consider your childhood to have been
a happy one? Why or why not?

_____

_____

_____

_____

_____

_____

_____

_____

What advice would you give to your teenage self today?

_____
_____
_____
_____
_____
_____
_____
_____
_____
_____
_____
_____
_____
_____
_____
_____
_____
_____
_____
_____
_____
_____
_____
_____
_____
_____
_____
_____

notes

•••

interests
& pursuits

Were you able to follow your career dreams, or did
circumstances dictate what work you had to do?

_____

_____

_____

_____

_____

_____

_____

_____

_____

_____

_____

_____

_____

_____

_____

Did you attend college, trade school, or join the
military? If so, when and where?

_____

_____

_____

_____

_____

_____

_____

What were the highlights of your post-high school experience?

_____
_____
_____
_____
_____
_____
_____
_____
_____
_____
_____
_____
_____
_____
_____

Do you have any regrets about your post-high school
experience? Would you have done anything differently?

_____
_____
_____
_____
_____
_____
_____
_____
_____
_____
_____
_____
_____
_____
_____

Do you have any general thoughts about education, training, or
military service that will be helpful to future generations?

_____

_____

_____

_____

_____

_____

_____

_____

_____

_____

_____

_____

_____

_____

_____

_____

_____

_____

_____

_____

_____

_____

_____

_____

_____

_____

_____

_____

_____

What was the first job you had where you earned a
paycheck? How old were you? Did you like it?

_____

_____

_____

_____

_____

_____

_____

_____

_____

_____

_____

_____

How did you get your first job?

_____

_____

_____

_____

_____

_____

_____

_____

_____

_____

_____

_____

_____

_____

_____

_____

Describe what jobs you have had since high school.

_____

_____

_____

_____

_____

_____

_____

_____

_____

_____

_____

_____

_____

_____

_____

_____

_____

What's the best job you've ever had? Why did you enjoy it?

_____

_____

_____

_____

_____

_____

_____

_____

_____

Where was the first place you lived when you left your
parents' home, and did you live there with others?

_____

_____

_____

_____

_____

_____

_____

_____

_____

_____

_____

_____

What's the most important thing you learned in school
that actually helped you in the real world?

_____

_____

_____

_____

_____

_____

_____

Who taught you how to drive?

_____

_____

_____

_____

_____

_____

_____

What pets have you had in your life? What were their names
and what are your fondest memories of them?

_____

_____

_____

_____

_____

_____

_____

_____

_____

_____

_____

_____

_____

_____

_____

What hobbies have you had, or do you have? When
did you start and how did you get into them?

_____

_____

_____

_____

_____

_____

_____

_____

_____

_____

Describe activities you love doing or that bring you joy.

_____

_____

_____

_____

_____

_____

_____

_____

_____

_____

_____

_____

_____

_____

_____

_____

_____

_____

_____

_____

_____

_____

_____

_____

_____

_____

_____

_____

_____

_____

notes

...

family tree

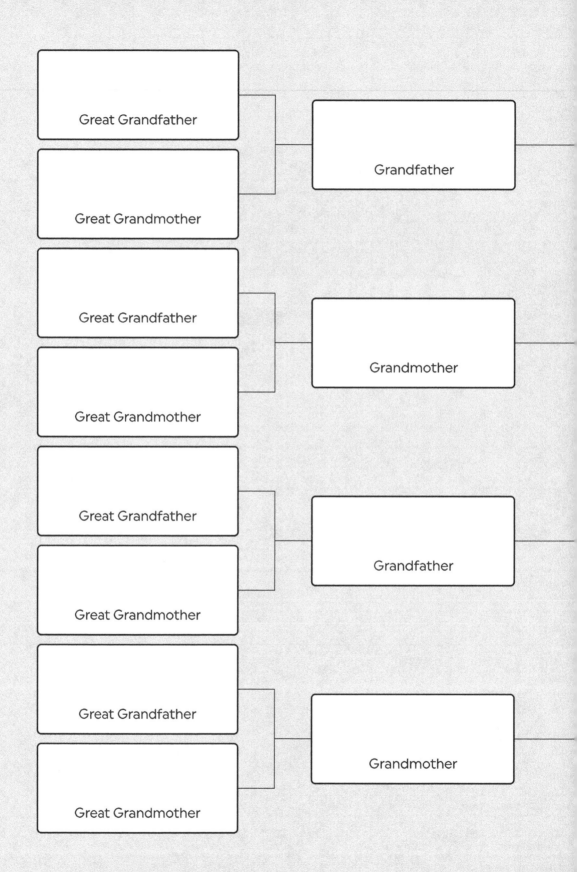

Great Grandfather

Great Grandmother

Grandfather

Great Grandfather

Great Grandmother

Grandmother

Great Grandfather

Great Grandmother

Grandfather

Great Grandfather

Great Grandmother

Grandmother

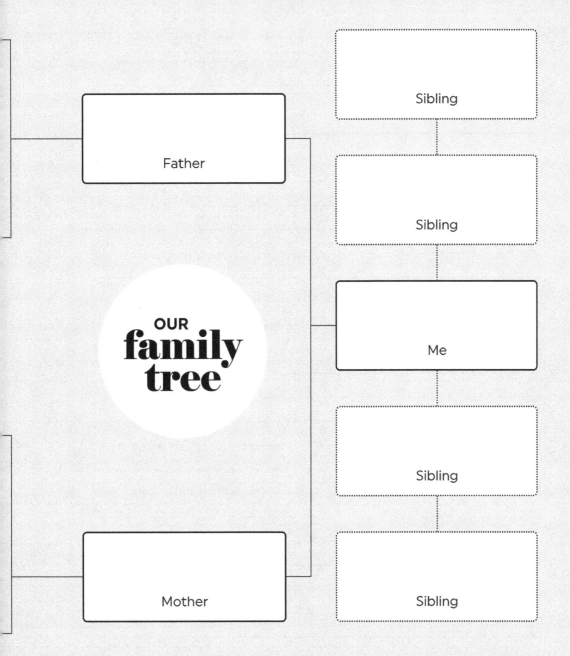

Father

Mother

OUR
**family
tree**

Sibling

Sibling

Me

Sibling

Sibling

notes

...

family, friends, & relationships

my parents

FIRST NAME

LAST NAME & MAIDEN NAME

DATE OF BIRTH

BIRTH PLACE

EYE COLOR

HAIR COLOR

OCCUPATION

FIRST NAME

LAST NAME & MAIDEN NAME

DATE OF BIRTH

BIRTH PLACE

EYE COLOR

HAIR COLOR

OCCUPATION

Describe your relationship with each (or either) of your parents while you were growing up. What was it like? How did your relationship change as you became an adult?

What was at least one important thing you learned to
do or appreciate from each of your parents?

_____

_____

_____

_____

_____

_____

_____

_____

_____

_____

_____

_____

_____

_____

_____

_____

_____

_____

_____

_____

_____

_____

_____

_____

_____

my siblings

FIRST NAME

LAST NAME & MAIDEN NAME

DATE OF BIRTH	BIRTH PLACE
EYE COLOR	HAIR COLOR

OCCUPATION

FIRST NAME

LAST NAME & MAIDEN NAME

DATE OF BIRTH	BIRTH PLACE
EYE COLOR	HAIR COLOR

OCCUPATION

FIRST NAME

LAST NAME & MAIDEN NAME

DATE OF BIRTH	BIRTH PLACE
EYE COLOR	HAIR COLOR

OCCUPATION

FIRST NAME

LAST NAME & MAIDEN NAME

DATE OF BIRTH	BIRTH PLACE
EYE COLOR	HAIR COLOR

OCCUPATION

Which traits do you share with your sibling(s), whether physical or character? In what way(s) do your traits differ?

_____

_____

_____

_____

_____

_____

_____

_____

_____

_____

_____

_____

_____

_____

_____

_____

_____

_____

_____

_____

_____

_____

_____

_____

Did you get along with your sibling(s) as a child?

_____

_____

_____

_____

_____

_____

_____

_____

_____

_____

_____

_____

In what way(s) has your relationship with your
sibling(s) changed over the years?

_____

_____

_____

_____

_____

_____

_____

_____

_____

_____

_____

_____

_____

my grandparents

FIRST NAME

LAST NAME & MAIDEN NAME

DATE OF BIRTH	BIRTH PLACE
EYE COLOR	HAIR COLOR

OCCUPATION

FIRST NAME

LAST NAME & MAIDEN NAME

DATE OF BIRTH	BIRTH PLACE
EYE COLOR	HAIR COLOR

OCCUPATION

FIRST NAME

LAST NAME & MAIDEN NAME

DATE OF BIRTH	BIRTH PLACE
EYE COLOR	HAIR COLOR

OCCUPATION

FIRST NAME

LAST NAME & MAIDEN NAME

DATE OF BIRTH	BIRTH PLACE
EYE COLOR	HAIR COLOR

OCCUPATION

What similar or different character traits or personality traits did you see in your grandparents compared to your parents?

_____

_____

_____

_____

_____

_____

_____

_____

_____

_____

_____

_____

_____

_____

_____

_____

_____

_____

_____

_____

_____

_____

_____

_____

_____

_____

_____

_____

How close are you or were you to your grandparents?
What memories or stories of them can you share?

_____

_____

_____

_____

_____

_____

_____

_____

_____

_____

_____

_____

_____

_____

_____

_____

_____

_____

_____

_____

_____

_____

_____

_____

_____

_____

_____

_____

What's an important lesson you were taught by
either or both of your grandparents?

_____

_____

_____

_____

_____

_____

_____

_____

_____

_____

_____

_____

_____

_____

_____

_____

_____

_____

_____

_____

_____

_____

_____

_____

_____

_____

_____

_____

_____

my children

FIRST NAME

LAST NAME & MAIDEN NAME

DATE OF BIRTH	BIRTH PLACE
EYE COLOR	HAIR COLOR

OCCUPATION

FIRST NAME

LAST NAME & MAIDEN NAME

DATE OF BIRTH	BIRTH PLACE
EYE COLOR	HAIR COLOR

OCCUPATION

FIRST NAME

LAST NAME & MAIDEN NAME

DATE OF BIRTH	BIRTH PLACE
EYE COLOR	HAIR COLOR

OCCUPATION

FIRST NAME

LAST NAME & MAIDEN NAME

DATE OF BIRTH	BIRTH PLACE
EYE COLOR	HAIR COLOR

OCCUPATION

Which character traits do you love about each child?

_____

_____

_____

_____

_____

_____

_____

_____

_____

_____

_____

_____

_____

_____

_____

_____

_____

_____

_____

_____

_____

_____

_____

_____

_____

_____

_____

_____

_____

What is your dream for your grandchildren and great-grandchildren

_____

_____

_____

_____

_____

_____

_____

_____

_____

_____

_____

_____

_____

_____

_____

_____

_____

_____

_____

_____

_____

_____

_____

_____

_____

_____

_____

_____

_____

family

Who do you have the most in common with in your
family? Who do you have the closest bond with?

_____

_____

_____

_____

_____

_____

_____

_____

_____

Have there ever been any serious arguments or fall-outs among your
family members? What caused them, and were they ever resolved?

_____

_____

_____

_____

_____

_____

_____

_____

_____

_____

_____

_____

_____

_____

_____

What are some interesting facts about your family? For example, famous people in your family tree, family lineage, the origin of your family's name, family antiques or heirlooms, etc

_____

_____

_____

_____

_____

_____

_____

_____

_____

_____

_____

_____

_____

_____

_____

_____

_____

_____

_____

_____

_____

_____

_____

_____

_____

_____

_____

_____

friends

Who are (or have been) your closest and dearest friends in
life, and what stories do you have of your friendships?

_____

_____

_____

_____

_____

_____

_____

_____

_____

_____

_____

_____

_____

_____

_____

_____

_____

_____

_____

_____

_____

_____

_____

_____

_____

_____

Who is your oldest friend and how many years have you been friends?

_____

_____

_____

_____

_____

_____

_____

_____

_____

_____

Describe a time when a friendship disappointed you
or caused you pain. Was there a resolution?

_____

_____

_____

_____

_____

_____

_____

_____

_____

_____

_____

_____

_____

_____

_____

Who do you (or did you) always go to for advice, and
what is a good example of their great advice?

_____

_____

_____

_____

_____

_____

_____

_____

_____

_____

_____

_____

_____

_____

_____

_____

_____

_____

_____

_____

_____

_____

_____

_____

_____

_____

_____

relationships

How old were you when you went on your first proper
date? Whom was it with and where did you go?

_____

_____

_____

_____

_____

_____

_____

_____

_____

_____

Do you have any personal love stories that you want to share?
For example, your first crush or a breakup story?

_____

_____

_____

_____

_____

_____

_____

_____

_____

_____

How and when did you meet your current partner?

_____

_____

_____

_____

_____

_____

_____

_____

_____

_____

_____

_____

_____

_____

_____

_____

_____

_____

_____

_____

_____

_____

_____

_____

_____

_____

_____

_____

_____

What qualities do you love most about your partner?

_____

_____

_____

_____

_____

_____

_____

_____

_____

_____

_____

_____

_____

_____

_____

_____

_____

_____

_____

_____

_____

_____

_____

_____

_____

_____

_____

_____

_____

_____

Did you have a wedding celebration? Describe the proposal, wedding day, and favorite memories of your wedding.

Based on your experiences, what relationship advice
would you like to pass on to future generations?

_____

_____

_____

_____

_____

_____

_____

_____

_____

_____

_____

_____

_____

_____

_____

_____

_____

_____

_____

_____

_____

_____

_____

_____

_____

_____

_____

notes

notes

fatherhood

Describe when you first knew you were going
to be a dad. How did you feel?

_____

_____

_____

_____

_____

_____

_____

_____

_____

_____

_____

What aspects of fatherhood created the biggest worries
for you, and how did this change over the years?

_____

_____

_____

_____

_____

_____

_____

_____

_____

_____

_____

_____

How did your upbringing influence the way you raised your children?

_____

_____

_____

_____

_____

_____

_____

_____

_____

_____

_____

_____

_____

_____

Did you plan to have the number of children you had? What was
a typical family size at the time of your own family planning?

_____

_____

_____

_____

_____

_____

_____

_____

_____

_____

_____

_____

_____

In what ways do you consider today's world to be a better place to raise children compared to your childhood days? In what ways is it more challenging to raise children today than it used to be?

_____

_____

_____

_____

_____

_____

_____

_____

_____

_____

_____

_____

_____

How old were you when you found out you were going to be a grandpa? Can you remember how you felt after hearing the news?

_____

_____

_____

_____

_____

_____

_____

_____

_____

_____

_____

_____

What is the best thing about being a grandpa? Are there any aspects of being a grandpa that are different from what your expectations were?

_____

_____

_____

_____

_____

_____

_____

_____

_____

_____

_____

_____

_____

_____

In what ways have you treated your grandchildren differently
than you treated your own children at the same age?

_____

_____

_____

_____

_____

_____

_____

_____

_____

_____

_____

_____

_____

_____

With hindsight, what advice would you give yourself
today as a new dad and as a parent?

_____

_____

_____

_____

_____

_____

_____

_____

_____

_____

_____

_____

_____

_____

_____

_____

_____

_____

_____

_____

_____

_____

_____

_____

_____

_____

notes

notes

•••

beliefs
& values

What were your parents' spiritual or religious beliefs and affiliations? Did they change over time? What influence have these had in your life? Have you maintained the same beliefs?

_____

_____

_____

_____

_____

_____

_____

_____

_____

_____

_____

_____

How have your spiritual or religious beliefs and affiliations evolved during your life?

_____

_____

_____

_____

_____

_____

_____

_____

_____

_____

_____

_____

_____

What makes you feel most patriotic (or not) about the land of your birth?

_____

_____

_____

_____

_____

_____

_____

What influences have shaped your political beliefs, and
have you always maintained the same beliefs?

_____

_____

_____

_____

_____

_____

_____

_____

_____

_____

_____

Did you grow up in an environment of traditional gender roles? Can you
remember how you felt about this? Do you share the same views today?

_____

_____

_____

_____

_____

_____

_____

_____

Are there any ways in which changes in your view of the world
have changed the way you live your life? (For example, recycling,
boycotting certain products, ditching certain habits etc.)

_____

_____

_____

_____

_____

_____

_____

_____

_____

_____

_____

Do you support any charities? If so, why are these causes important to you?

_____

_____

_____

_____

_____

_____

_____

_____

_____

_____

_____

_____

_____

_____

_____

_____

What do you consider to be your core values in life? What values do you most want to pass on to future generations in your family?

_____

_____

_____

_____

_____

_____

_____

_____

_____

_____

_____

_____

_____

_____

_____

_____

_____

_____

_____

_____

_____

_____

_____

_____

_____

_____

_____

_____

_____

_____

notes

...

reflections

How would you describe yourself?

_____

_____

_____

_____

_____

_____

_____

_____

_____

_____

_____

_____

_____

_____

_____

_____

_____

_____

_____

_____

_____

_____

_____

_____

_____

_____

_____

_____

Is there anything in your family's medical history that
your children or grandchildren should know?

_____

_____

_____

_____

_____

_____

_____

_____

_____

_____

What does success mean to you? Who are some
people you believe are successful?

_____

_____

_____

_____

_____

_____

_____

_____

_____

_____

_____

_____

_____

_____

_____

_____

_____

_____

Do you have a favorite age or stage in your life?

_____

_____

_____

_____

_____

_____

_____

_____

Who has been the most influential person in your
life? In what ways have they influenced you?

_____

_____

_____

_____

_____

_____

_____

_____

_____

_____

_____

_____

_____

_____

_____

_____

_____

_____

Looking back, what do you wish you'd made more time for?

_____

_____

_____

_____

_____

_____

_____

_____

_____

_____

What's one of the most important lessons you've learned about people?

_____

_____

_____

_____

_____

_____

_____

_____

_____

_____

_____

_____

_____

_____

_____

_____

_____

_____

What lessons have you learned about money that you would
like to pass on to your children and future generations?

_____

_____

_____

_____

_____

_____

_____

_____

_____

_____

_____

With hindsight, what advice would you give to younger
generations today about home ownership?

_____

_____

_____

_____

_____

_____

_____

_____

_____

_____

_____

_____

_____

Excluding your children, what do you consider to have
been your greatest achievement in life so far?

_____

_____

_____

_____

_____

_____

_____

_____

_____

_____

_____

_____

_____

_____

_____

_____

_____

_____

_____

_____

_____

_____

_____

_____

_____

_____

_____

_____

_____

_____

_____

Do you have any regrets in your life? Do you still
hope you will be able to make them right?

_____

_____

_____

_____

_____

_____

_____

_____

_____

_____

_____

_____

Have any events or happenings that you thought were
major issues turned out to be blessings in disguise?

_____

_____

_____

_____

_____

_____

_____

_____

_____

_____

_____

_____

_____

Has anything happened in your lifetime (personal or global)
that you hope future generations never go through?

_____

_____

_____

_____

_____

_____

_____

_____

_____

What's one of the most stressful times you've had to
endure in your life and how did you handle it?

_____

_____

_____

_____

_____

_____

_____

_____

_____

_____

_____

_____

_____

_____

Describe a scary moment in your life. How did you overcome
this and what did you learn from the experience?

_____

_____

_____

_____

_____

_____

_____

_____

_____

_____

_____

Is there anything you've experienced in your life that you think
everyone should experience? If so, what, and for what reasons?

_____

_____

_____

_____

_____

_____

_____

_____

_____

_____

_____

_____

What are some of the most amazing experiences
that have happened to you?

_____

_____

_____

_____

_____

_____

_____

_____

_____

_____

_____

_____

_____

_____

_____

_____

_____

_____

_____

_____

_____

_____

_____

_____

_____

_____

_____

_____

What is one trait you have that you would most like to improve upon?

_____

_____

_____

_____

_____

_____

_____

_____

_____

_____

_____

_____

What secrets do you believe help to create a fulfilling life?

_____

_____

_____

_____

_____

_____

_____

_____

_____

_____

_____

_____

_____

_____

What's the best advice you've received?

_____

_____

_____

_____

_____

_____

_____

_____

_____

_____

_____

_____

_____

_____

_____

_____

_____

_____

_____

_____

_____

_____

_____

_____

_____

_____

_____

_____

_____

_____

What would you want your great-grandchildren and
future generations to know about you?

_____

_____

_____

_____

_____

_____

_____

_____

_____

_____

_____

_____

_____

_____

_____

_____

_____

_____

_____

_____

_____

_____

_____

_____

_____

_____

_____

From your experiences, what life lessons or advice
would you want to share with others?

_____

_____

_____

_____

_____

_____

_____

_____

_____

_____

_____

_____

_____

_____

_____

_____

_____

_____

_____

_____

_____

_____

_____

_____

_____

_____

_____

_____

_____

notes

_____
_____
_____
_____
_____
_____
_____
_____
_____
_____
_____
_____
_____
_____
_____
_____
_____
_____
_____
_____
_____
_____
_____
_____
_____
_____
_____

...

short questions

my firsts

What was your first word?

How old were you when you had your first kiss?

When was the first time you fell in love?

What was the first movie you saw in a movie theater?

At what age did you first try alcohol?

How old were you when you first drove a car?

What make and model was your first car? Did you name it?

What was the first record (or tape, CD, or another format) you bought?

Which artist/band was playing at the first concert you went to?

Where did you go on your first vacation without your parents?

Where did you go for your first job interview?

Who was the first non-family member you cooked a meal for?

When and where was your first car ding or fender bender?

Where did you go on your first airplane flight?

What's the first country you visited outside your birth country?

my top five...

Most memorable places you've visited

1. _____
2. _____
3. _____
4. _____
5. _____

Best attributes

1. _____
2. _____
3. _____
4. _____
5. _____

Most listened to singers, bands or musicians?

1. _____
2. _____
3. _____
4. _____
5. _____

Pieces of advice you would give your 16-year-old self

1. _____
2. _____
3. _____
4. _____
5. _____

Famous people (dead or alive) you would most like to meet

1. _____
2. _____
3. _____
4. _____
5. _____

Favorite ice cream flavors

1. _____
2. _____
3. _____
4. _____
5. _____

Things you would do if you had a multi-million-dollar lottery win

1. _____
2. _____
3. _____
4. _____
5. _____

Best presents you remember receiving

1. _____
2. _____
3. _____
4. _____
5. _____

my favorite...

COLOR	BBQ FOOD
MOVIE SNACK	BOOK
HOT DRINK	SPORT TO PLAY AND/OR WATCH
SEASON OF THE YEAR	BOARD OR CARD GAME
WAY TO SPEND A SUNDAY	BEDTIME STORY AS A CHILD
CANDY OR CHOCOLATE BAR	RESTAURANT AND ITEM ON THE MENU
ACTOR OR ACTRESS	MOVIE
WAY TO UNWIND AFTER A HARD DAY	COCKTAIL OR NON-ALCOHOLIC DRINK
CITY YOU'VE VISITED	ANNUAL CELEBRATION, EXCLUDING YOUR BIRTHDAY
DESSERT OR CAKE	SMELL

quick questions

Do you have a lucky number? If so, what is it?

_____

_____

_____

What type of weather do you love most?

_____

_____

_____

Do you have a valid passport?

_____

_____

_____

What food do you like to have made for you when you're sick?

_____

_____

_____

Are you a morning person or an evening person?

_____

_____

_____

Do you buy lottery tickets? If so, do you always choose the same numbers?

_____

_____

_____

If you could snap your fingers and become an expert
in something, what would you want it to be?

_____

_____

_____

_____

Who or what can always make you laugh?

_____

_____

_____

If you were granted three wishes, what would they be?

_____

_____

_____

What simple pleasures of life do you truly enjoy?

_____

_____

_____

_____

Have you ever won any competition prizes?

_____

_____

_____

What is the most expensive or extravagant thing you have ever bought?

_____

_____

_____

_____

Where did you go on the longest road trip you've ever been on?

_____

_____

_____

_____

What is the farthest you have ever traveled?

_____

_____

_____

_____

Are you superstitious?

_____

_____

_____

What is one of your worst habits?

_____

_____

_____

_____

Do you prefer to be spontaneous or think things through first?

_____

_____

_____

Have you ever broken any bones?

_____

_____

_____

What do you procrastinate over most?

_____

_____

_____

Do you believe in fate?

_____

_____

_____

What in life do you consider to be a waste of money?

_____

_____

_____

_____

_____

_____

What is the most romantic thing anyone has ever done for you?

_____

_____

_____

_____

Do you have a favorite proverb or inspirational
quote that you like to live by?

_____

_____

_____

_____

_____

What makes a birthday special for you?

_____

_____

_____

_____

_____

What famous or important people have you encountered
in real life and how did you meet them?

_____

_____

_____

_____

What is your ideal vacation?

_____

_____

_____

_____

_____

Describe your dream home. Where is it? How
big is it? What features does it have?

_____

_____

_____

_____

_____

_____

_____

List the cities you've lived in throughout your life so far.

_____

_____

_____

_____

_____

_____

_____

_____

_____

_____

_____

_____

List the top ten places on your bucket list you would visit
if resources (money and time) were not a concern.

_____

_____

_____

_____

_____

_____

_____

_____

_____

_____

_____

_____

...

notes to loved ones

notes to loved ones

THIS IS A SPACE FOR YOU TO WRITE NOTES TO YOUR LOVED ONES

notes to loved ones

_____
_____
_____
_____
_____
_____
_____
_____
_____
_____
_____
_____
_____
_____
_____
_____
_____
_____
_____
_____
_____
_____
_____
_____
_____
_____
_____
_____
_____
_____
_____

notes to loved ones

_____

_____

_____

_____

_____

_____

_____

_____

_____

_____

_____

_____

_____

_____

_____

_____

_____

_____

_____

_____

_____

_____

_____

_____

_____

_____

_____

_____

notes to loved ones

notes to loved ones

_____
_____
_____
_____
_____
_____
_____
_____
_____
_____
_____
_____
_____
_____
_____
_____
_____
_____
_____
_____
_____
_____
_____
_____
_____
_____
_____
_____
_____
_____
_____
_____

About Us

We're an odd bunch of fun, quirky, and creative authors who love writing thought-provoking questions.

We've all experienced awkward silence situations and resorted to superficial chitchat and small talk to pass time.

The authors here at Questions About Me are on a mission to end dull conversations. We created the *Questions About Me* series to invigorate conversations and help you get to know people better—including yourself.

The *Tell Me Your Life Story* series helps capture your experiences, life stories, and reflections into a timeless keepsake to share with your children, loved ones, and future generations.

Put down your phone, switch off the TV, and use our books to unlock endless conversational possibilities, develop deeper relationships, and create precious memories.

www.questionsaboutme.com

Also by Questions About Me

TELL ME YOUR LIFE STORY SERIES

Tell Me Your Life Story, Mom
Tell Me Your Life Story, Dad
Tell Me Your Life Story, Grandma
Tell Me Your Life Story, Grandpa

QUESTIONS ABOUT ME SERIES

3000 Unique Questions About Me
2000 Unique Questions About Me
1000 Unique Questions About Me

3000 Would You Rather Questions About Me
2000 Would You Rather Questions About Me
1000 Would You Rather Questions About Me